Contents

Welcome

1 **Match.**

① ② ③ ④ ⑤ ⑥

And I'm Hoopla.

I'm Harry. I'm nine.

My name's Hip.

I'm Professor Bloom.

I'm Hop.

My name's Rose.

2 **Draw and write about yourself.**

Hello.

My name's _____.

I'm (age) _____.

3 **Write.**

1 My name's _____Hip_____ .

2 My name's _____ .

3 I'm _____. I'm _____.

4 I'm _____.

5 I'm Professor _____ .

6 I'm _____.

4 1:05 **Listen and write.**

Hey boys! Hey _____girls_____!

Come with us, come on a quest today!

_____ up, down, here, there.

Look around everywhere.

Where's the _____?

Come on, come on.

Come on a quest!

Let's find the _____!

5 🔊 1;09 **Listen and write.**

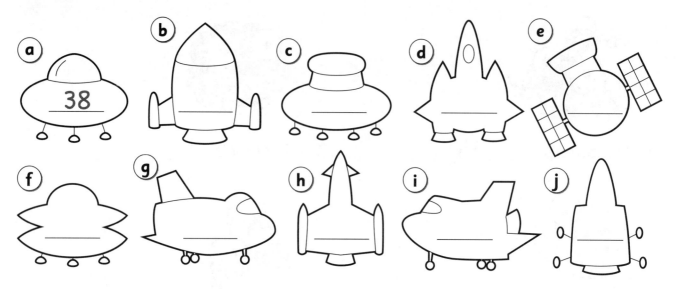

a ____38____

b _____

c _____

d _____

e _____

f _____

g _____

h _____

i _____

j _____

6 🔊 1:10 **Listen and write.**

1 There are ____thirty-three____ birds in the tree.

2 There are _____ horses in the stable.

3 There are _____ tables in the classroom.

4 There are _____ teachers in the school.

5 There are _____ children at the party.

7 **Write.**

a	21	24	27	30	33
b	33	35	37		41
c	20			35	40
d	10	20	30		
e			39	44	49
f	18	20			26

8 (1:13) **Listen, write and match.**

1 Boris _Wednesday_

2 Billy _____

3 Jenny _____

4 Marie _____

5 Andy _____

6 Mike _____

7 Judy _____

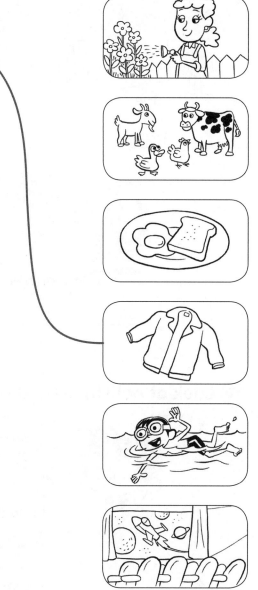

9 **What's your favourite day? Write.**

_____ favourite day?

My _____ is _____.

10 Unscramble and write the months.

1 Joe — HCAMR — 31

2 Jenny — PEBMESTRE — 6

3 Peter — RNBEOMVE — 10

March _____ _____

4 Ann and Pam — NJUE — 17

5 Rover — YAJUNAR — 25

_____ _____

11 Look at Activity 10 and write.

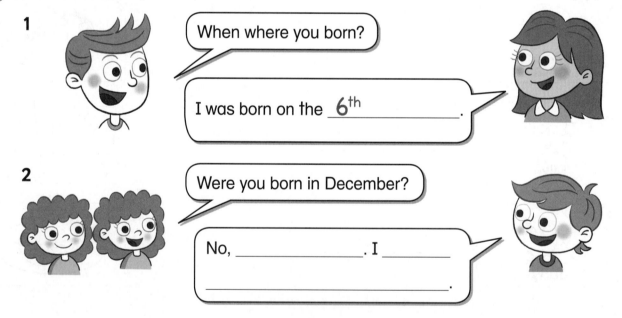

1 When where you born?

I was born on the __6th_____.

2 Were you born in December?

No, _____. I _____
_____.

12 Write about a friend.

_____ was born in _____.

He/She is _____ years old.

13 (1:17) **Listen and circle the correct days.**

Sunday	Monday	Tuesday	Wednesday	Thursday	Friday	Saturday
	(1st)	2nd	3rd	4th	5th	6th
7th	8th	9th	10th	11th	12th	13th
14th	15th	16th	17th	18th	19th	20th
21st	22nd	23rd	24th	25th	26th	27th
28th	29th	30th	31st			

A U G U S T

14 **Write the dates.**

1 fifteenth of May: _15th of May_

2 twenty-second of September: _____

3 first of April: _____

4 twentieth of August: _____

5 twelfth of January: _____

6 seventeenth of March: _____

7 twenty-third of December: _____

15 **Look and write.**

1 Were you born in May?
   No, I wasn't. I was born _____.

2 Were you born on the first day of the week?

   _____

3 Were you born on the 18th of January?

   _____

1 Nature

1 **Write. Then colour.**

| flowers | sun | insects | birds | mushrooms |
| clouds | pond | rock | animal | trees |

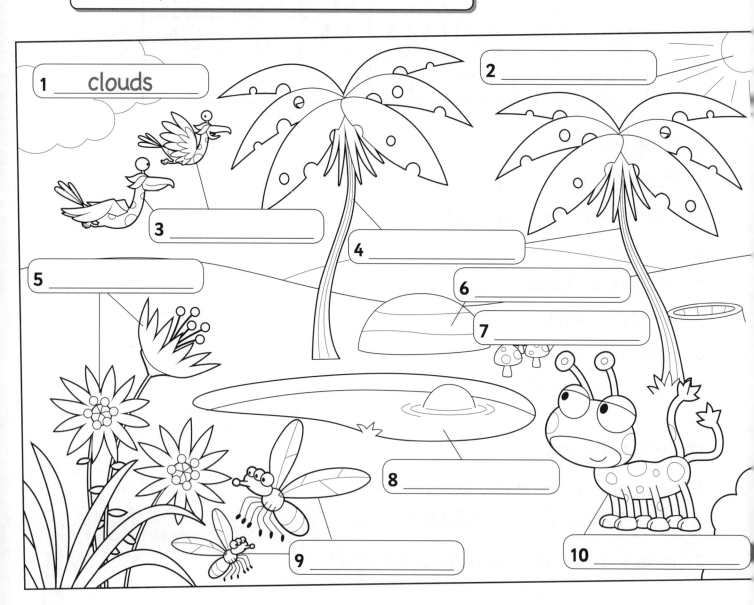

1 ____clouds____

2 _____

3 _____

4 _____

5 _____

6 _____

7 _____

8 _____

9 _____

10 _____

2 (1:22) **Listen, colour and draw.**

3 **Look at Activity 2 and write.**

1 How many ponds are there? There's <u>one blue pond</u>.

2 How many flowers are there? There are _____.

3 How many rocks are there? _____ brown _____.

4 How many birds are there? _____ blue _____.

5 How many insects are there? _____

6 How many animals are there? _____

4 **Look and write.**

ants butterflies rainbow roses sky spiders wind worms

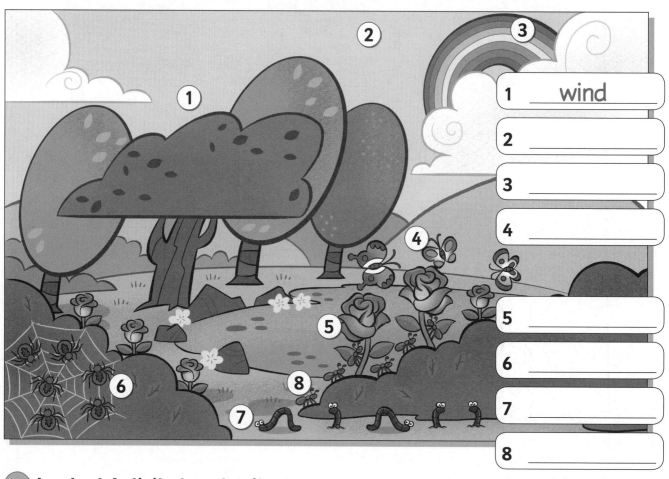

1 ___wind___

2 _____

3 _____

4 _____

5 _____

6 _____

7 _____

8 _____

5 **Look at Activity 4 and write.**

1 There ___are___ ___six___ ants.

2 There _____ _____ rainbow.

3 There _____ _____ worms.

4 There _____ _____ butterflies.

5 There _____ _____ roses.

6 _____ _____ _____ spiders.

7 _____ _____ _____ trees.

8 _____ _____ _____ clouds.

6 Read. Then draw and colour.

There is a big blue pond. There are three green trees.
There are some pink insects. There are four yellow birds.
There is a rainbow. There aren't any butterflies. There isn't any wind.

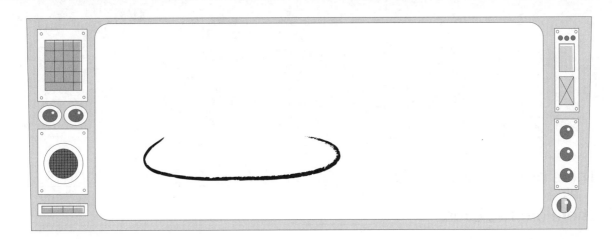

7 Listen and tick (✓).

1

2

3

4

8 Find and write the sentences.

1 they / are / where   Where are they?

2 the / park / at   _____

3 is / where / he   _____

4 museum / the / at   _____

9 Read the story again. Where is Hoopla? Write.

_____

10 Find the mistakes and write.

1 There are (two) mushrooms.   There are three mushrooms.

2 There are two birds.   _____

3 There's a flower.   _____

4 There are insects.   _____

5 There's a rock.   _____

11 Number the pictures in order.

12 Write.

1 They are _____.

2 Rose likes the aliens' _____.

13 **Read the words. Circle the pictures.**

chair   hair   pair   tear

PHONICS

air   ear

14 🔊 1:31 **Listen and connect the letters. Then write.**

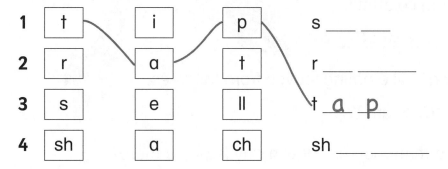

1   t   i   p   s __ __

2   r   a   t   r __ __

3   s   e   ll   t _a_ _p_

4   sh   a   ch   sh __ __

15 🔊 1:32 **Listen and write the words.**

1   f _air_   2 __ __   3 __ __   4 __ __

16 🔊 1:33 **Read aloud. Then listen and check.**

There is a boy on the bed. His hair is a mess. There is a pair of socks near the chair.

17 **Draw and write.**

 +  = 6

 – = 4

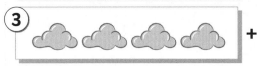 + = 7

 – = 2

1   Four insects plus _____two insects_____ equals six.

2   Seven mushrooms minus _____ equals four.

3   Four clouds plus _____ equals seven.

4   Six flowers minus _____ equals two.

18 **Read and write.**

1   I am a biped animal. I am colourful.
    I can fly. What am I? _____parrot_____

2   I am a quadruped animal. I like eating leaves from tall trees.
    I've got very long legs. What am I? _____

3   There are two birds and three horses. How many legs are there? _____

4   There are two dogs and three snakes. How many legs are there? _____

19 **Write the numbers.**

a   11 + __2__ = 13   **b**   20 – ____ = 13

c   12 + ____ = 13   **d**   18 – ____ = 13

Wider World

20 **Read and write *T* = *True* or *F* = *False*.**

1 Pablo and Lucy live in Spain. F

2 Lucy plays board games at the weekend.

3 Pablo plays with sandcastles in the summer.

4 Lucy lives near the sea.

21 **Look, read and tick (✓).**

Where do you play?

1 In the playground

2 On the beach

3 At home

22 **Write about yourself.**

I'm _____.

I'm from _____.

I live _____.

I play _____.

Unit Review

23 Look and write.

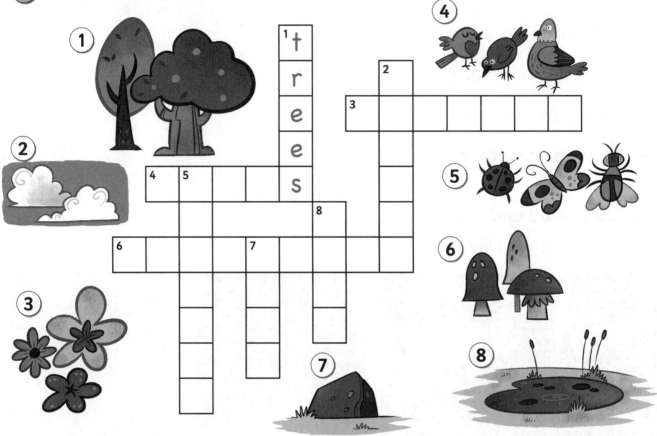

Crossword puzzle:
- 1 (down): t r e e s
- 3 (across)
- 2 (down)
- 4 (across) / 5 (down)
- 8 (down)
- 6 (across) / 7 (down)

24 Look and write.

There's …

1 _____ a rock _____.

2 _____

3 _____

There are some …

4 _____

5 _____

6 _____

About Me

25 Look and write.

1 Are there any <u>insects</u> in the tree?

Yes, there are _____ in the tree.

2 How many _____ are on the rock?

_____ one _____ .

3 Is there any wind or rain?

No, _____ _____ .

26 Write about your favourite place.

My favourite place is _____ .

There's _____ . There are _____ .

There isn't _____ . There aren't _____ .

 I can describe nature. ☐

I can solve Maths problems. ☐

2 Me

1 🔘 1:40 **Listen and colour. Then match.**

small nose

white moustache ⟶ (Grandad)

short beard ⟶ (Mum)

green eyes (Peter)

blond hair

blue eyes

small glasses

red hair

grey hair

thick eyebrows

2 **Look at Activity 1 and write.**

1 Grandad has got a short _____beard_____, a _____ moustache and _____ eyebrows.

2 Mum has got blond _____ and a _____ nose.

3 Peter _____ nose and _____ hair.

4 Grandad _____ hair, green _____ and small _____.

5 Mum and Peter have got _____.

3 Choose, draw and colour. Then write.

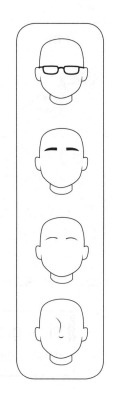

I've got _____ and _____.

I haven't got _____.

4 Look and write.

| He's got   He hasn't got   She's got   She hasn't got |

1 __He's got__ thick eyebrows.

2 _____ long hair.

3 _____ big glasses.

4 _____ a beard.

5 _____ a small nose.

6 _____ long hair.

7 _____ glasses.

8 _____ black hair.

5 🔘 1:45 **Listen and number.**

a Tom	**b** Sally	**c** John	**d** Mary
		 1	

6 **Look at Activity 5 and write.**

> strong arms   strong legs   long eyelashes
> long neck   round chin   short fingernails

1 John hasn't got _short fingernails_____.

2 Mary has got a _____.

3 Tom has got _____.

He hasn't got _____.

4 Sally has got a _____.

She hasn't got _____.

7 **Write about your family.**

1 My _____ has got _____.

_____ hasn't got _____.

2 My _____ has got _____.

_____ hasn't got _____.

3 My _____ has got _____.

_____ hasn't got _____.

Lesson 3 vocabulary (describing your body)

8 🔘 1:48 **Listen and tick (✓). Then write.**

1

2

3

He's got _____ hair and _____ arms. He hasn't got _____.

9 **Read. Then write.**

My name's Meesoo. I'm **10** years old. I love swimming and dancing. I've got black hair and thin eyebrows. I've got strong arms and legs. I've got a flat stomach. I haven't got broad shoulders. I haven't got glasses.

1 Has she got blond hair? _____ No, she hasn't. _____

2 Has she got thin eyebrows? _____

3 Has she got strong legs and arms? _____

4 Has she got glasses? _____

5 Has she got broad shoulders? _____

10 **Write about a friend.**

Friend's name: _____

1 Has _____ got glasses? _____

2 _____? No, _____ hasn't.

3 _____? Yes, _____ has.

11 Read the story again. Is Hip's new friend an alien or a monster? Write.

_____

12 Number the pictures.

1 He's got a long neck.　　　**2** He's got a round chin.

3 He's got big teeth.　　　　**4** He's got a big nose.

13 Number the pictures in order.

14 Find the mistakes and write.

1 Hip's new friend has got (ten) eyes.

　　Hip's new friend has got two eyes.

2 Hip's friend is horrible.

_____

3 Hip's new friend is from the train.

_____

15 **Read the words. Circle the pictures.**

ay   er

say   dinner   letter   play

16 (1:53) **Listen and connect the letters. Then write.**

1	d	i	d	p ___ ___
2	s	a	s	th ___ ___
3	p	a	t	d _a_ _d_
4	th	i	th	s ___ ___

17 (1:54) **Listen and write the words.**

1 s ay   2 ___ ___   3 ___ ___ ___   4 ___ ___ ___

18 (1:55) **Read aloud. Then listen and check.**

Dad has his dinner. Mum has got a letter. The girl plays with the dog.

19 **Look and match.**

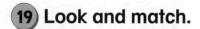

1

man

woman

men

women

people

black eyes

long neck

black hair

big nose

round chin

2

3

4

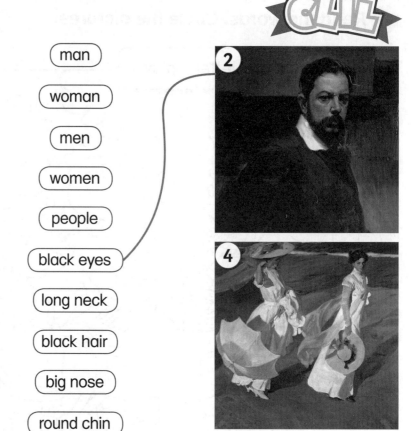

20 **Draw a portrait. Then circle and write.**

(There's a / There are) _____ in my painting.

(He's / She's / They've) got _____.

(He hasn't / She hasn't / They haven't) got _____.

Wider World

21 **Read and write** *T = True* **or** *F = False*.

1   Martin has got two sisters.   T

2   His mother has got grey hair.

3   Fatima has got a brother.

4   Her father has got a moustache.

22 **Draw a portrait of your family. Write.**

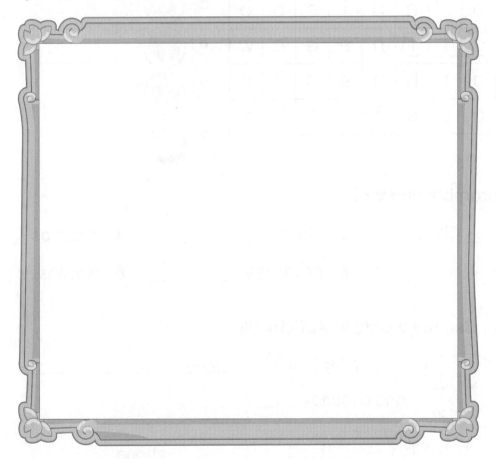

I've got _____.

My _____ has got _____.

My _____ has got _____.

Unit Review

23 **Find, circle and write.**

t	e	e	t	h	p	s	b	e
u	m	o	u	s	t	a	e	y
g	l	a	s	s	e	s	a	e
l	n	o	p	e	m	n	r	b
o	s	r	a	c	s	o	d	r
p	o	t	a	p	i	s	o	o
h	a	i	r	h	e	e	e	w
c	a	r	b	n	e	c	k	s
m	o	u	s	t	a	c	h	e

1   hair

2   _____

3   _____

4   _____

5   _____

6   _____

7   _____

8   _____

24 **Unscramble and write.**

1 nich ___chin___   **2** sthec _____   **3** mahctos _____

4 msra _____   **5** hsudolres _____   **6** aleeshsey _____

25 **Write. Use the words in Activity 24.**

1 __She's got__ long _____

and a round _____.

2 _____ strong _____

and a flat _____.

3  _____ broad _____

and a strong _____.

About Me

26 Look and write.

1 ____chin____

2 _____

3 _____

4 _____

5 _____

6 _____

27 Look at Activity 26 and write.

1  Has she got long eyelashes? _____No, she hasn't._____

2 Has he got a black moustache? _____

3  Has she got short fingernails? _____

4 Has he got a strong chest? _____

28 Write about a friend or family member.

My _____ has got _____ and

_____.

He/She hasn't got _____.

 I can describe physical appearance. ☐
I can look for information. ☐

3 Pets

1 **Look and write.**

beak   claws   feathers   fins   fur   paws   tail   wings

feathers _____   _____   _____   _____

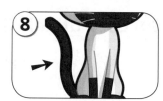

_____   _____   _____   _____

2 **Look and write.**

cat   parrot   wings   rabbit   skin   snake   whiskers   paws

1

We've got a 🐱 and a 🐍 . Our _____ cat _____ has got long _____.

Our _____ has got green and brown _____.

2

We've got a and a 🦜 . Our _____ has got white

_____ . Our _____ has got two _____.

3 **Look and write.**

| has got   hasn't got   have got   haven't got |

 **1**

What ___does___ it look like? _____ two eyes.

_____ legs

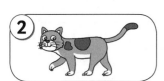 **2**

_____ does it _____ like?

_____ a tail. _____ arms.

 **3**

What do _____ look _____?

_____ claws. _____ fur.

4 **Look and write.**

1 The rabbit has got ___paws___ and _____ .

2 The parrot has got two _____ and a _____.

3 The cat hasn't got _____.

4 The dog has got _____.

5 The snake hasn't got _____.

6 The frog has got green _____. It hasn't got _____.

7 The fish has got _____.

Lesson 2 grammar (*What does it look like? It's got/hasn't got ...*)

29

5 (1:66) **Listen and draw. Then write.**

1 The tortoise has got a
hard shell .

2 The cat has got
_____ .

3 The eagle has got
_____ .

4 The dog has got
_____ .

6 **Match.**

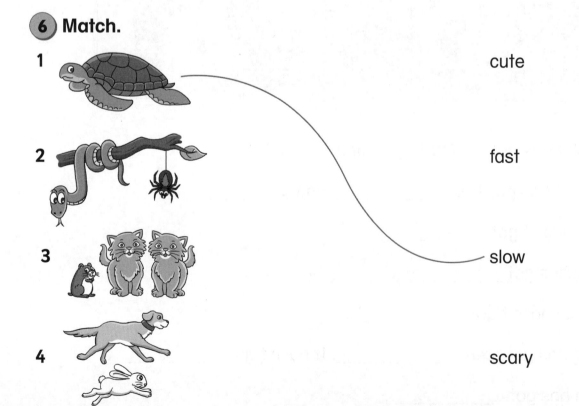

1   cute

2   fast

3   slow

4   scary

7   **Listen and circle. Then write.**

Animal: cat / (rabbit)

Name: Luke / Lily

Age: 3 years old / 8 years old

Colour: white / brown

Legs: no legs / four legs

Food: eggs / vegetables

I've got a pet. It's a ¹_____rabbit_____ but it doesn't look like a rabbit. Its

name is ²_____. It's ³_____ years old. It's ⁴_____

and round like a ball. It's got thick, long fur. It's got two eyes and

⁵_____ legs but you can't see them. There's a lot of fur!

It's got a cage with ⁶_____, water and toys.

8 **Look at Activity 7 and write.**

What __does it__ look like?

Has it got fins?

_____ a hard shell?

Has it got _____?

_____ is it?

_____, it _____.

_____, it _____.

_____, it _____.

It's thick and long.

It's a _____.

9 Read the story again. What animals can you find in the story? Write.

_____

10 Look and write.

1. This animal has got __whiskers__ and long ears.

2. This animal has got _____ and a beak.

3. This animal has got smooth _____. It _____ legs.

4. This animal has got fur, a long _____ and _____ legs.

11 Read and tick (✓).

This animal has got spotty skin and six legs. It's got glasses.

① ☐ ② ☐ ③ ☐

12 Read the words. Circle the pictures.

coin eat leaf tea

13 (1:72) Listen and connect the letters. Then write.

1 [c]   [i]   [k]   r _____ _____

2 [d]   [a]   [ng]   c _a_ _p_

3 [r]   [n]   [p]   d _____ _____

4 [i]   [i]   [g]   i _____ _____

14 (1:73) Listen and write the words.

1 _p_ _ea_ _ch_   2 _____ _____ _____   3 _____ _____ _____   4 _____ _____ _____

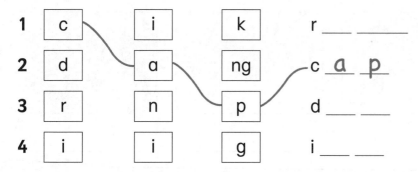

15 (1:74) Read aloud. Then listen and check.

Join me for tea. We can have leaf tea in a cup. We can eat too.

16 **Number the pictures in order. Then write.**

Life cycle of the butterfly

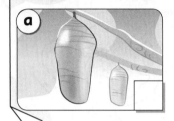  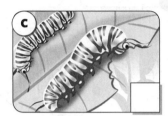 

| butterflies | caterpillars | cocoons | eggs |

First there are small ___eggs___ . Then there _____ .

Then _____ . Finally _____ .

17 **Look and write.**

| big tadpoles | eggs | frogs | small tadpoles |

Life cycle of a frog

___eggs___ _____

18 **Write.**

1 Have butterflies got wings? ___Yes, they have.___

2 Have frogs got big mouths? _____

3 Have small tadpoles got legs? _____

4 Have caterpillars got legs? _____

Wider World

19 **Read and match. Then find one difference.**

1 She's got a short tail.

2 She's got a small head.

(a)

(b)

3 She's got small ears.   **4** She's got long ears.   **5** She's got fur.

20 **Draw your favourite pet. Write.**

I've got a _____. His/Her name is _____.

It's got _____.

He/She likes _____.

Unit Review

21 Unscramble and write.

skewhirs ginsw ruf tila wacsl kins sifn aftershe swap beka

1 ___whiskers___ 2 _____

3 _____ 4 _____

5 _____ 6 _____

7 _____ 8 _____

9 _____ 10 _____

22 Look and tick (✓).

	Fast	Slow	Smooth skin	Soft fur	Hard shell
Hamster	✓			✓	
Tortoise					
Frog					

23 Look at Activity 22 and write.

1 The hamster is _____fast_____. It's got _____

   but it hasn't got _____.

2 The tortoise is _____. _____

3 The frog _____. _____

About Me

24 Draw and label two animals.

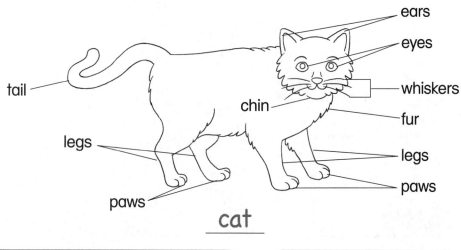

ears

eyes

whiskers

fur

tail

chin

legs

legs

paws

paws

<u>cat</u>

_____   _____

25 Choose an animal in Activity 24 and write.

The _____ has got _____ and _____ but it

hasn't got _____.

26 Write about your favourite pet.

My favorite pet is a _____. It is _____.

It's got _____ but it hasn't got _____.

 I can talk and write about pets. ☐

I can understand and make diagrams. ☐

4 Home

1 **Match.**

wardrobe   mirror

plant

picture

bin

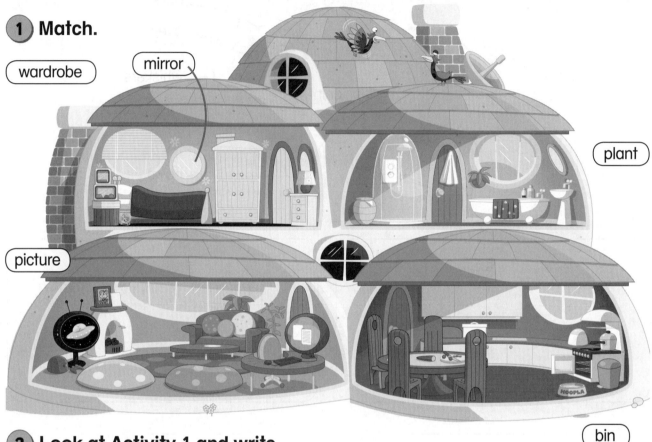

2 **Look at Activity 1 and write.**

> opposite   behind   above   below   in front of   next to

1 The sofa is <u>in front of</u> the plant.

2 The sofa is _____ the small table.

3 The bin is _____ the cooker.

4 The bath is _____ the window.

5 The mirror is _____ the sink.

6 The wardrobe is _____ the bed.

7 The chair is _____ the cooker.

3 Look and write *T* = *True* or *F* = *False*.

1   There are pictures in the bedroom. They're above the bed   **T**

2   There's a plant in the living room. It's behind the sofa.   ☐

3   There's a bin in the kitchen. It's in front of the fridge.   ☐

4   There's a cooker in the kitchen. It's next to the sink.   ☐

5   There's a mirror in the bathroom. It's above the sink.   ☐

6   There's a lamp in the bedroom. It's next to the bed.   ☐

7   There's a frog in the bathroom. It's in the sink.   ☐

4 Read. Draw the items in the picture in Activity 3.

1   There's a plant in the bathroom. It's opposite the shower.

2   There's a wardrobe in the bedroom. It's next to the bed.

3   There's a lamp in the living room. It's behind the sofa.

4   There's a picture in the kitchen. It's above the sink.

5 **Look and write.**

blanket   broom   comb   cupboard   pans   pots   plates   towels

1 Is the ___comb___ on the cooker?   Yes, it is.

2 Are the _____ in the bath?   Yes, they are.

3 Are the _____ in the kitchen?   Yes, they are.

4 Is the _____ in front of the sofa?   Yes, it is.

5 Are the _____ in the sink?   No, they aren't. They're on the table.

6 Are the _____ in the cupboard?   No, they aren't. They're on the sofa.

7 Is the _____ behind the sink?   No, it isn't. It's in front of the TV.

8 Is the _____ in the kitchen?   Yes, it is.

6 (2:08) **Listen and write.**

1 __Yes__, it __is__.   **2** _____, they _____.   **3** _____, it _____.

4 _____, it _____.   **5** _____, it _____.   **6** _____, it _____.

7 **Look and write.**

bed   chair   computer   in front of   next to   plant   sofa   under

1 Is the hamster in the shower? _____ Yes, it is. _____

2 Is the hamster on the bed? _____

3 Is the hamster on the sofa? _____

4 _____ behind the _____? Yes, it is.

5 _____ in front of the _____? No, it isn't.

It's above the chair.

6 Is the hamster under the computer? _____

_____

8 (2:09) **Look at Activity 7. Then listen and write the number.**

a [3]   b [ ]   c [ ]   d [ ]   e [ ]   f [ ]

Lesson 4 grammar (*Is the broom in the wardrobe?*)

9 Read the story again. Is Hoopla a hamster? Write.

_____

10 Number the pictures in order.

a Hoopla's got ...?

b No, no, ...

c Hoopla's got ....

d

e My hamster's got .... | 1 |

11 Write *T = True* or *F = False*.

1 Hip's hamster has got a TV. | T |

2 Hip's hamster's TV is in the living room. | |

3 Hoopla's got a TV. | |

4 Hoopla is behind the wheel. | |

12 Write.

big
hamster
Hoopla's
wheel

Hoopla's got a ___hamster___ wheel?

No, no, it isn't a _____ _____ ! _____
got a _____ _____ !

13 **Read the words. Circle the pictures.**

bone   cake   home   time

14 (2:14) **Listen and connect the letters. Then write.**

1	k	i	t	t ____ __
2	t	ee	l	k _i_ _ck_
3	k	ai	ck	f ____ __
4	f	i	d	k __ __

15 (2:15) **Listen and write the words.**

1 w_ave_   2 ____ ____   3 __ __

4 __ ____   5 __ __

16 (2:16) **Read aloud. Then listen and check.**

The boy eats his cake and the dog has got a bone. It's time to go home but the park is fun.

17 **Find and colour the frog.**

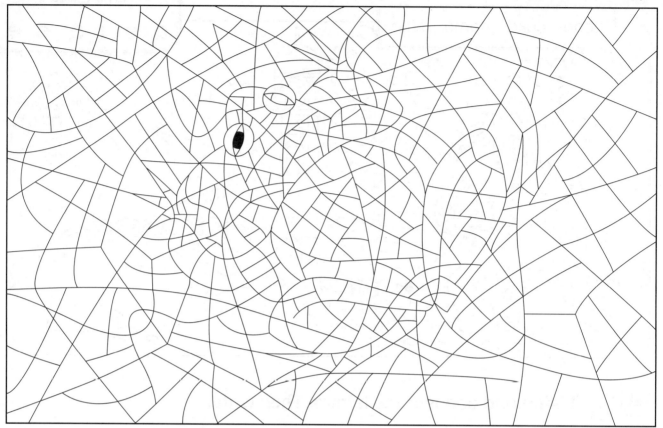

18 **Write. Then draw a mosaic animal.**

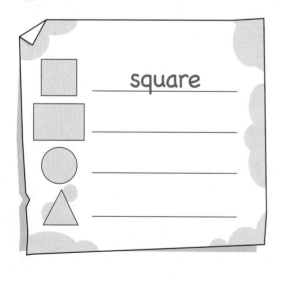

square

_____

_____

_____

19 **Write three things we can use to make mosaics.**

1 _____   2 _____   3 _____

Wider World

20 **Read and match.**

pizza

pillow

game

teddy bear

book

pyjamas

21 **Read and write _T = True_ or _F = False_.**

What do you do at a sleepover party?

1	Stay with a friend.	T
2	Have pillow fights.	
3	Go to bed early.	
4	Tell stories.	
5	Wear your uniform.	
6	Play games.	

22 **Write about a sleepover party.**

My name's _____. I'm from _____.

At my sleepover party we eat _____.

We wear _____. Then we _____.

Unit Review

23 **Unscramble and write.**

1 empcourt   *computer*   2 ebrawrdo _____

3 adupborc _____   4 omorb _____

5 bocm _____   6 urbshototh _____

7 epalts _____   8 ewolts _____

9 kenbalts _____   10 sapn _____

24 (2:19) **Listen and draw. Then write.**

1 There are ___*towels*___ in the bathroom. They're _____ the sink.

2 There's a bed _____ the _____.

3 Is there a lamp behind the sofa? _____.

4 Is there a wardrobe in the bedroom? _____.

5 There are _____ in the living room.

   They're _____ the sofa.

6 Is there a mirror above the sink? _____.

About Me

25 Draw and colour a room in your house.

26 Write about the room in Activity 25.

My living room is great! There is a big sofa. There is a small table in front of the sofa. There is a big green plant. The TV is opposite the plant. There is a computer on the big table behind the sofa. There are pictures on the wall.

My _____ is _____. There is _____

_____. There is _____.

The _____ is _____ the _____. There is _____

_____. There are _____.

27 Write questions about your house.

1 Is there _____ opposite the _____? Yes, there is.

2 Are there _____ above the _____? No, there aren't.

3 _____ below the _____? No, there isn't.

4 _____ in front of the _____? Yes, there is.

I CAN I can describe my home. ☐
           I can find information with help from someone. ☐

TEACHER

5 Clothes

1 Match.

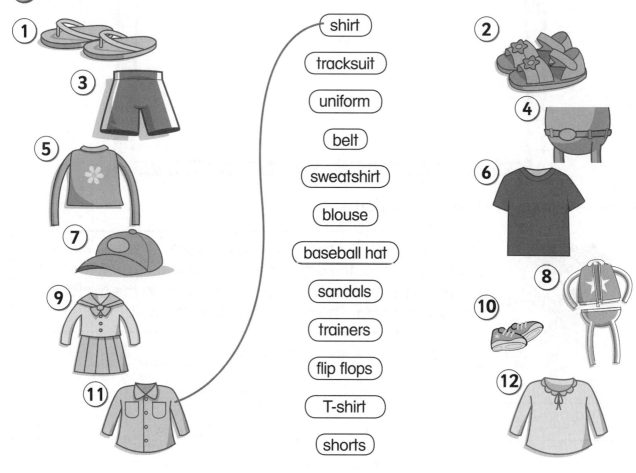

1
3
5
7
9
11

shirt
tracksuit
uniform
belt
sweatshirt
blouse
baseball hat
sandals
trainers
flip flops
T-shirt
shorts

2
4
6
8
10
12

2 Look and write.

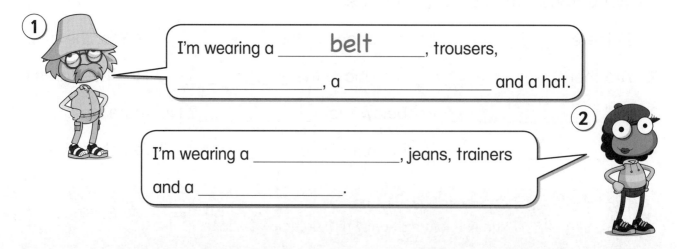

1
I'm wearing a _____ belt _____, trousers,
_____, a _____ and a hat.

2
I'm wearing a _____, jeans, trainers
and a _____.

48   Lesson 1 vocabulary (clothes)

3 2:25 **Listen and draw. Then colour.**

What's Harry wearing?

He's wearing …

4 **Look at Activity 3 and write.**

1 What's he wearing? He's wearing a ___baseball hat___ , a _____ ,
   _____ and _____ .

2 Is he wearing a belt? _____ , he _____ .

3 Is he wearing a baseball hat? _____ , he _____ .

5 **Write. Then listen and colour.**

> beanie   hiking boots   scarf   ski jacket   tights   woolly jumper

1 ___beanie___

2 _____

3 _____

4 _____

5 _____

6 _____

6 **Look at Activity 5 and write.**

> colourful   fancy   leather   plain

1 Is ___she___ wearing a _____ woolly jumper?
   No, _____.

2 _____ wearing a _____ ski jacket.

3 _____ wearing a _____ beanie.

4 Is _____ wearing _____ shoes? Yes, _____.

7 (2:30) **Look and tick (✓). Then listen and circle.**

shoes ☐	baseball hat ☐
trainers ✓	belt ☐
blouse ☐	skirt ☐
sweatshirt ☐	jeans ☐
glasses ☐	shorts ☐

1 Yes, she is. / ⟨No, she isn't.⟩   **2** Yes, she is. / No, she isn't.

3 Yes, she is. / No, she isn't.   **4** Yes, she is. / No, she isn't.

8 **Write.**

my favourite   These are   I love   This is

1 _These are_ my favourite hiking boots. _____ my favourite jumper.

2 _____ my tights and my leather shoes! This is _____ scarf.

9 **Tick (✓) your favourite clothes.**

a baseball hat ☐	a ski jacket ☐	a sweatshirt ☐
a beanie ☐	a blouse ☐	blue jeans ☐
a belt ☐	a uniform ☐	a T-shirt ☐
sandals ☐	flip flops ☐	shorts ☐

10 Read the story again. Is Hop wearing red trousers?

Write. _____

11 Look and write. Then number the pictures in order.

my T-shirt   my favourite hat   my favourite trainers   my new coat

a

Do you like ___my T-shirt___ ?

Look! I'm wearing _____
_____.

b

c

I'm wearing _____
_____.

Ha ha! It's _____
_____.

d

12 Look and write.

glasses   jeans   shorts
scarf   T-shirt

1 Is Harry wearing trousers? _No, he isn't. He's wearing shorts._

2 Is Rose wearing a tracksuit? _____
_____

3 Is Hop wearing a long coat? _____

4 Is Hoopla wearing a baseball hat? _____
_____

Lesson 5 story and values (Be polite!)

13 **Read the words. Circle the pictures.**

scarf   skate   spoon   star

sc	sk	sm	sn
sp	squ	st	sw

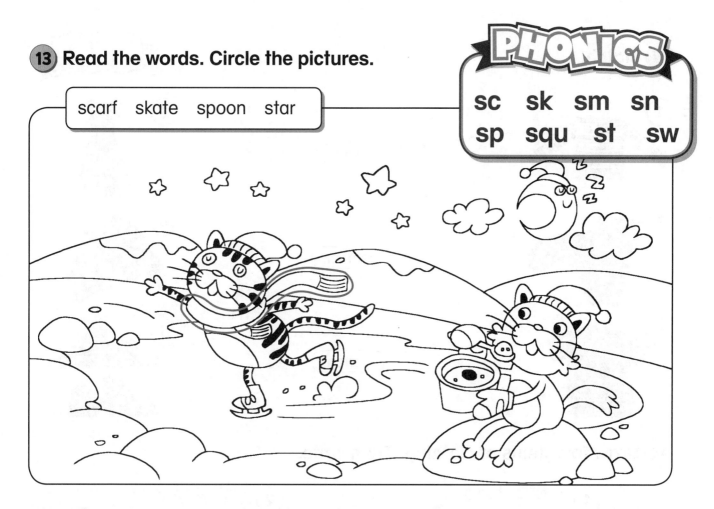

14 (2:35) **Listen and connect the letters. Then write.**

1	h	u	t	c _____ ___
2	c	igh	t	c ___ ___
3	l	oa	t	h _a_ _t_
4	c	a	p	l _____ ___

15 (2:36) **Listen and write the words.**

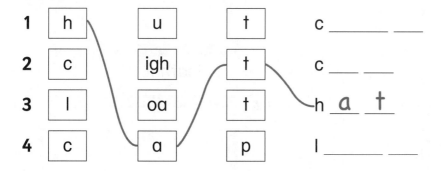

1 __sm__ _e_ _ll_   2 _____   3 _____   4 _____

16 (2:37) **Read aloud. Then listen and check.**

The cats skate on the lake. One wears a hat and one wears a scarf.
The moon is high and we can see a big star.

17 **Match.**

1

wool

2

3

leather

4

5

cotton

6

18 **Draw four items of clothing. Then write.**

1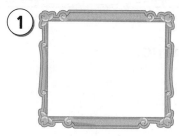

wool

2

leather

3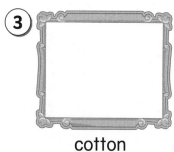

cotton

4

polyester

1 The _____ is made from wool.

2 The _____ made from _____.

3 The _____ cotton.

4 The _____.

Wider World

19 **Read and colour.**

1 My name's Clara and I'm from Mexico. In my school we don't wear a uniform. Here, I'm wearing black trousers, a plain red T-shirt and my favourite trainers. They're black and very comfortable.

2 My name's Jiaming. I'm from China. We wear a uniform in my school. I'm wearing blue shorts, a white shirt, grey socks and brown sandals. These are my favourite sandals.

20 **Read and write _T = True_ or _F = False_.**

1 Clara is wearing a uniform. `F`

2 Clara is wearing her favourite trainers. ☐

3 Clara is not wearing black trousers. ☐

4 Jiaming is wearing shorts. ☐

5 Jiaming is not wearing a uniform. ☐

6 Jiaming is wearing his favourite sandals. ☐

21 **Describe what you are wearing.**

I'm wearing _____.

I'm not wearing _____.

Unit Review

22 **Find and circle the words.**

d	a	d	s	m	b	e	a	n	i	e	j	s	s
b	e	l	m	o	a	s	u	b	j	s	o	k	a
s	w	e	a	t	s	h	i	r	t	h	c	i	n
u	b	h	j	z	e	o	n	o	e	o	n	j	d
n	l	a	a	b	b	r	i	o	a	r	p	a	a
i	s	s	t	r	a	c	k	s	u	i	t	c	l
f	w	c	c	s	l	s	s	t	n	b	l	k	s
o	e	a	k	a	l	q	h	s	t	l	o	e	y
r	a	r	e	s	h	a	o	f	i	o	s	t	m
m	b	e	l	t	a	u	r	s	g	u	h	w	c
s	b	l	t	o	t	u	t	e	h	s	i	x	i
c	w	s	c	a	r	f	s	a	t	e	r	t	b
f	l	i	p	f	l	o	p	s	s	c	t	b	o
w	o	o	l	l	y	j	u	m	p	e	r	r	n

23 **Write the questions or answers.**

1 Is he wearing trainers?

   No, he isn't. He's wearing hiking boots .

2 _____?

   Yes, he is. It's his favourite T-shirt.

3 Is he wearing trousers?

   _____.

4 _____?

   Yes, he is. He loves his baseball hat.

About Me

24 **Draw and colour your favourite clothes.**

25 **Write about your favourite clothes.**

These are my favourite trainers. They're _____.

This is my favourite baseball hat. It's _____.

I love my _____. _____ fancy.

_____. _____ colourful.

_____. _____ plain.

_____. _____ leather.

26 **Pretend you're wearing your favourite clothes. Write.**

Today I'm wearing _____

_____.

I CAN   I can talk about clothes.   ☐
         I can make lists.   ☐

TEACHER

6 Sports

1 Look and number.

1 jump
2 play basketball
3 run
4 climb trees
5 ride a bike
6 catch a ball
7 play badminton
8 do taekwondo
9 play football
10 play tennis

2 Read and circle.

1 I (can / can't) jump.

2 I (can / can't) climb trees.

3 I (can / can't) play badminton.

4 I (can / can't) play football.

5 I (can / can't) play basketball.

6 I (can / can't) ride a bike.

7 I (can / can't) do taekwondo.

8 I (can / can't) play tennis.

9 I (can / can't) run.

10 I (can / can't) catch a ball.

3 (2:46) **Listen and write ✓ = can or ✗ = can't.**

Jake						✓
Paul						
Beth						
Gina						
Max						

4 **Look at Activity 3 and write.**

1   He can _____ play football _____ but he can't
_____ .

2   She can _____ but she can't
_____ .

3   _____ but he can't
_____ .

4   Can he _____ ?
No, _____ .

5   _____ ?
Yes, _____ .

Lesson 2 grammar (*I can/can't run. / Can he/she play tennis?*)

5 Match the sports and places.

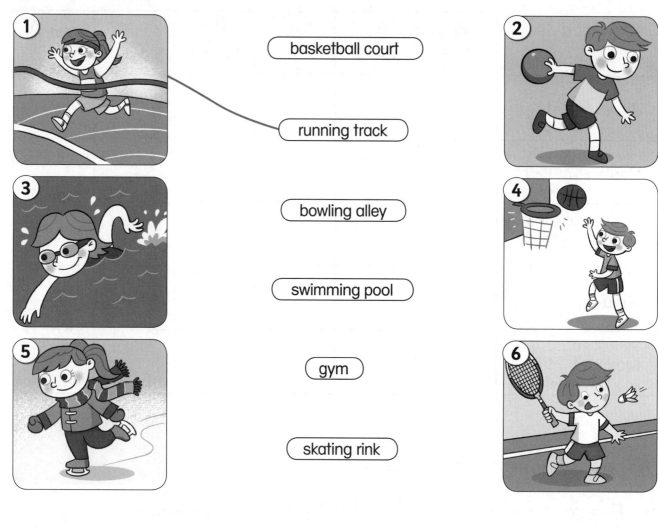

1

basketball court

running track

bowling alley

swimming pool

gym

skating rink

2

3

4

5

6

6 (2:49) Listen and tick (✓).

1

2

3

7 (2:50) Listen and write ✓ = *was* or ✗ = *wasn't*.

| **1** | running track | ✗ | **2** | basketball court | | **3** | gym | |
| | bowling alley | | | skating rink | | | ski slope | |

8 Look and write ✓ = *can* or ✗ = *can't*.

 1 ✓

 2

 3

 4

 5

 6

 7

8

9 Look at Activity 8. Write *and* or *but*.

Monkeys can run _____and_____ jump _____ they can't ride a bike.

They can swim _____ climb trees _____ they can't play tennis.

They can skate but they can't play football.

10 Look at Activity 8 and write.

 1 He wasn't at the bowling alley. He _____was_____ at the
____running track____.

 2 He _____ at the swimming pool. He _____ at
the _____.

 3 He _____ basketball court. He _____
_____.

 4 _____ skating rink. _____
_____.

5 _____ ski slope. _____
_____.

11 Read the story again. What can Hoopla do? Write.

_____

12 Look and write. Then tick (✓) the things that Hoopla can do.

> catch a ball   climb a tree   play football   play tennis
> read   ride a bike   run   swim

swim   run ✓

_____   _____

_____   _____

_____   _____

13 Look at Activity 12 and write.

1 Hoopla can't swim but he can run.

2 _____

3 _____

4 _____

14 **Read the words. Circle the pictures.**

flag   glass   sleep   slip

| bl | fl | gl |
| pl | sl | |

15 (2:56) **Listen and connect the letters. Then write.**

1 | p | | e | | k | b _____ __

2 | b | | oo | | ll | p u ff

3 | f | | u | | d | b _____ __

4 | b | | oo | | ff | f _____ __

16 (2:57) **Listen and write the words.**

1 bl a ck   2 _____   3 _____   4 _____

17 (2:58) **Read aloud. Then listen and check.**

Look at the ship with the black flag. One man slips.
Look out for that shark!

18 (2:60) **Listen and number.**

a

b

c

d

e

1

19 **Make an exercise plan. Write.**

catch a ball   climb   dance   do taekwondo   play badminton   play basketball
play football   play tennis   ride my bike   run   swim

My exercise plan

Monday		Friday	
Tuesday		Saturday	
Wednesday		Sunday	
Thursday			

20 **Write about your exercise plan.**

On Monday I can _____, on Tuesday I can _____,

_____

_____

_____

Wider World

21 **Look and write.**

cricket pitch   baseball field   a baseball bat and ball
a cricket bat and a ball   a cricket team   a baseball team

1
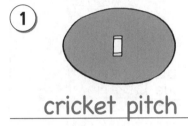
cricket pitch

2
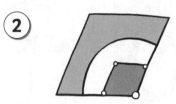
_____

3

_____

4

_____

5

_____

6
_____

22 **Look at Activity 21 and write.**

1 This _____ pitch _____ is round.

2 A _____ is also called a 'diamond'.

3 You play cricket with _____.

4 You play baseball with _____.

5 A _____ team has got _____ players.

6 A _____ team has got _____.

23 **Write about a popular team sport.**

_____ is a popular sport in _____. There are

_____ teams. There are _____ players in each team.

Unit Review

24 Look and write ✓ = *can* or ✗ = *can't*.

Ted

Sue

Lee

Liz

25 Look at Activity 24 and write.

1 Can Ted play baseball and ride a bike? <u>He can't play baseball</u>
<u>but he can ride a bike.</u>

2 Can Sue play tennis and basketball? _____

_____

3 Can Lee _____ and _____ ? _____

_____

4 Can Liz _____ ? _____

_____

About Me

26 **Write names of activities you can and can't do.**

I can	I can't

27 **Look at Activity 26 and write.**

1   I can _____ but I can't _____.

2   _____

3   _____

28 **Find and write the questions. Then answer about yourself.**

1   you / trees / can / climb

_____   _____

2   bike / you / ride / can / a

_____   _____

   I can talk about sports.

I can talk about my abilities.

7 Food

1 **Match.**

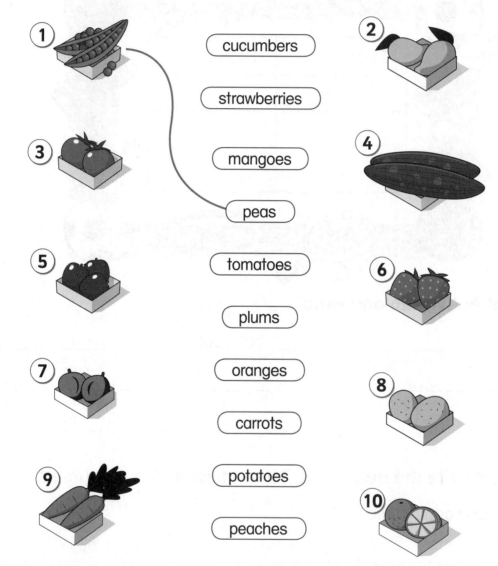

1 · peas

cucumbers

strawberries

mangoes

peas

tomatoes

plums

oranges

carrots

potatoes

peaches

2 **Write about the food that you like and don't like.**

😊 I like _____ .

☹ I don't like _____ .

3 🔘 3:06 **Listen and write ✓ = *likes* or ✗ = *doesn't like*.**

4 **Look at Activity 3 and write.**

1 Does she like strawberries?

___Yes, she does.___

2 Does she _____ plums?

_____

3 _____ she _____ peas?

_____

4 _____ he _____ cucumbers?

_____

5 _____ beans?

_____

6 _____ tomatoes?

_____

5 **Look and write Y = Yes or N = No.**

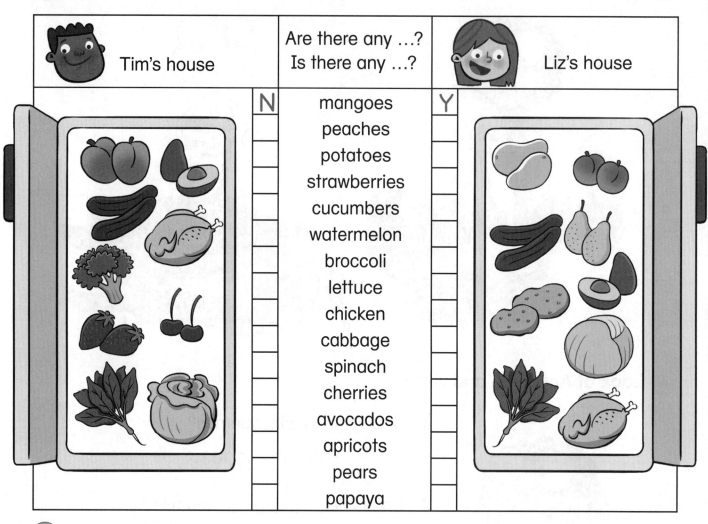

	Tim's house		Are there any ...? Is there any ...?		Liz's house
		N	mangoes	Y	
			peaches		
			potatoes		
			strawberries		
			cucumbers		
			watermelon		
			broccoli		
			lettuce		
			chicken		
			cabbage		
			spinach		
			cherries		
			avocados		
			apricots		
			pears		
			papaya		

6 **Look at Activity 5 and write.**

Tim's house

1 Are there any pears?

   No, there aren't.

2 Are there any cherries?

3 Is there any spinach?

4 Is there any lettuce?

Liz's house

1 Are there any avocados?

2 Are there any papayas?

3 Is there any cabbage?

4 Is there any broccoli?

7 (3:10) **Listen and draw a happy face or a sad face.**

8 **Look at Activity 7 and write.**

1 Does he like cereal? _____Yes, he does._____

2 Does he like strawberries? _____

3 Does he like eggs and toast? _____

4 Does he like peaches? _____

5 _____ bananas? Yes, he does.

6 _____ avocados? No, he doesn't.

9 **Draw food items. Then write your own questions and answers.**

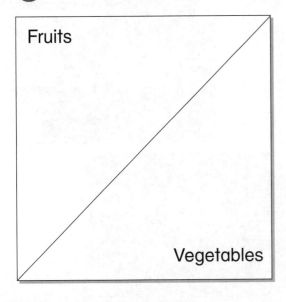

Fruits

Vegetables

1 Are there any _____? Yes, there are.

2 Is there any _____? No, there isn't.

3 Are there lots of _____?

_____

4 Is there a lot of _____?

_____

5 _____? Yes, there are.

6 _____? No, there aren't.

10 Read the story again. What colour foods can Hip and Hop eat? Write.

_____

11 Look and write.

Does she like ice cream?

_____ Yes, she does. _____

Does he like _____?

_____

Does she like strawberries?

_____

Does he like _____?

_____

12 Number the pictures in order.

72

Lesson 5 story and values (Stay healthy. Eat more fruit and vegetables.)

13 **Read the words. Circle the pictures.**

crab   frog   string   train

br   cr   dr   fr
gr   pr   str   tr

PHONICS

14 (3:15) **Listen and connect the letters. Then write.**

1   k   ar   ss   w ___ ___

2   w   i   k   g ___ ___ ___

3   sh   e   l   sh ___ ___ ___

4   g   ir   b   k _i_ _ss_

15 (3:16) **Listen and write the words.**

1   _br_ _ow_ _n_   2 ___ ___ ___   3 ___ ___ ___   4 ___ ___ ___

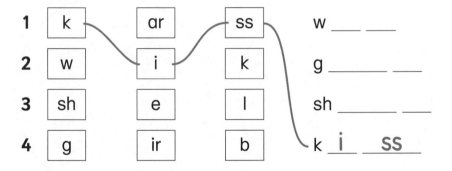

16 (3:17) **Read aloud. Then listen and check.**

The boy likes his toy train. He can pull it with the string. He's got a green frog, a brown owl and a red crab.

Lesson 6 phonics (br / cr / dr / fr / gr / pr / str / tr)   **73**

17 Match.

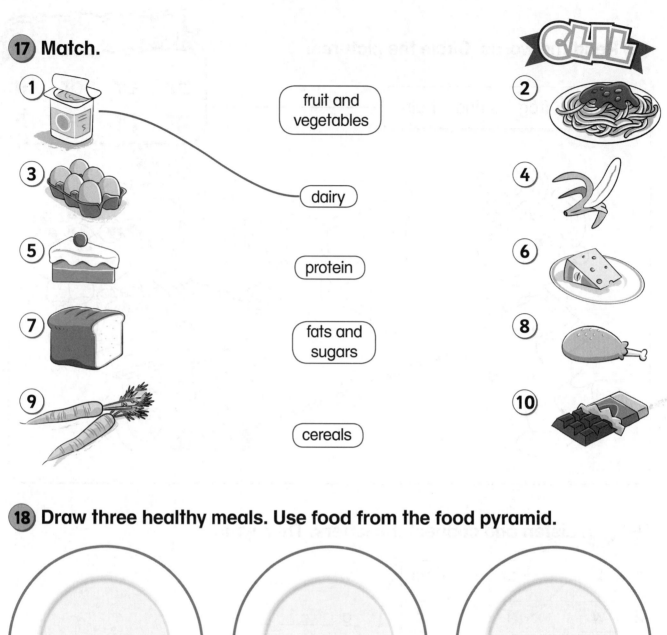

fruit and vegetables

dairy

protein

fats and sugars

cereals

18 Draw three healthy meals. Use food from the food pyramid.

breakfast   lunch   dinner

19 Look at Activity 18 and write.

For breakfast, I like _____.

For lunch, I like _____.

For dinner, I like _____.

Wider World

20 **Read and answer.**

1

I'm Andrea. I'm from Argentina. I don't like potatoes but I like meat. My favourite dinner is *asado* or barbecue. I also like chocolate sandwiches for a snack. They aren't healthy but they are very tasty!

My name's Zeki and I'm from Turkey. Here, I eat fantastic pastries and pistachios, almonds and walnuts. I love them. I also like chicken and fruit but I don't like kebabs.

2

1 Does Andrea like barbecue?   Yes, she does.

2 Are chocolate sandwiches healthy? _____

3 Does Zeki like kebabs?   _____

4 Does Zeki like fruit?   _____

21 **Write about food from your country.**

My name's _____.

I'm from _____.

I like _____ but I don't like _____.

My favourite dinner is _____.

_____ healthy.

Unit Review

22 Look and write.

Across →

1
2
3
4
5
6
7

Down ↓

2
4
6
8

¹t o m a t o e s

23 Look and write.

1 Does he like mangoes? ___Yes, he does.___

2 _____ strawberries?

_____

3 Does she like apricots? _____

4 _____ spinach?

_____

About Me

24 **Draw food items.**

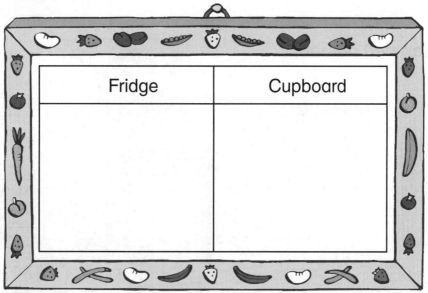

25 **Look at Activity 24 and write.**

1 There is some _____.

2 There are some _____.

3 There is a lot of _____.

4 There are lots of_____.

5 Is there any cereal? _____

6 Are there any strawberries? _____

26 **Write about your family.**

My mum likes _____. So do I. She doesn't like _____.

My dad likes _____. Me too. He doesn't _____.

 I can talk about foods. ☐

I can talk about likes and dislikes. ☐

8 Things we do

1 🔊 3:24 **Listen and number.**

2 **Look at Activity 1 and write.**

> cleaning   dancing   doing homework
> eating   sleeping   walking

Picture 1 _____eating_____.   Picture 3 _____.

Picture 6 _____.   Picture 8 _____.

Picture 9 _____.   Picture 10 _____.

3 (3:26) **Listen and match.**

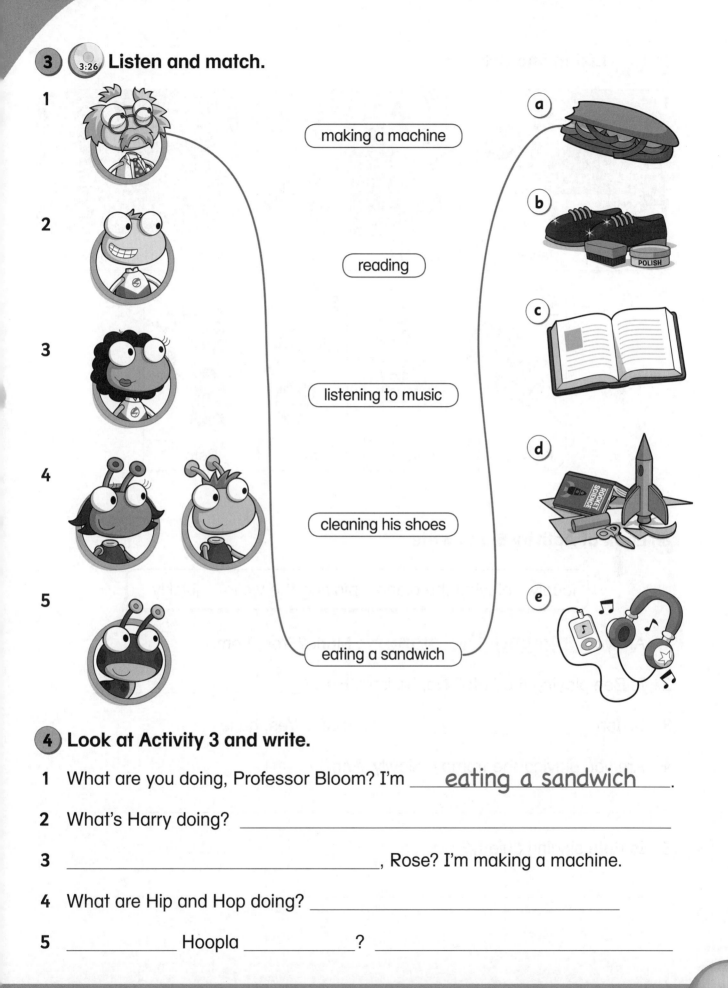

1 making a machine

2 reading

3 listening to music

4 cleaning his shoes

5 eating a sandwich

a
b
c
d
e

4 **Look at Activity 3 and write.**

1 What are you doing, Professor Bloom? I'm _____eating a sandwich_____.

2 What's Harry doing? _____

3 _____, Rose? I'm making a machine.

4 What are Hip and Hop doing? _____

5 _____ Hoopla _____? _____

5 (3:29) **Listen and tick (✓).**

Marie ☐   Jenny ✓

Ken ☐   Ben ☐

Karl ☐   Jon ☐

Kelly ☐   Ann ☐

Tim ☐   Pete ☐

6 **Look at Activity 5 and write.**

> loudly   playing the piano   playing the violin   quickly

1 Are you __playing the piano__ , Marie? Yes, I am.

2 Is Ben playing the flute? No, he isn't. He's _____ .

3 Is Jon _____ terribly? Yes, he is.

4 Are you playing the trumpet slowly, Ann?

   _____

5 Is Pete singing quietly?

   _____

7 **Listen and write.**

Hi, Jason!

I'm in Thailand now. I'm having fun but it's very hot!

I'm ¹ _eating_ a sandwich by the pool. My

sister is swimming ² _____ and my mum is

reading ³ _____. My dad is ⁴ _____

to music and singing ⁵ _____. But he's funny.

See you soon!

Bye,
Adam

To: Jason Spade

  10 Park Street

  New York

  NY 10013

  United States

8 **Look and write.**

playing the piano   quickly   reading   walking

_____Is he_____ sleeping?

No, _____. _____.

Is _____?

Yes, _____.

Is _____ slowly?

No, _____. _____

9 Read the story again. Who is helping Professor Bloom fix the machine? Write.

_____

10 Look and write.

1

What _____ is he _____ doing?

_____ fixing the machine.

2

What _____?

He's running.

3

Where _____ going?

They're _____ to Earth.

11 Look and write.

| ball   catching   drinking   eating   machines   reading   sandwich |

Hi, Hip. I'm ¹ _____ eating _____ a ² _____. Rose is ³ _____ and Professor Bloom is ⁴ _____ about ⁵ _____. Oh, and my dog is ⁶ _____ a ⁷ _____. What are you doing?

12 **Read the words. Circle the pictures.**

bump   hand   paint   wind

13 (3:35) **Listen and connect the letters. Then write.**

1	qu	e	z	b _ _ _
2	y	i	zz	y _ _ _
3	b	ow	n	qu _i_ _z_
4	d	u	s	d _ _ _ _

14 (3:36) **Listen and write the words.**

1 _a_ _sk_   2 _ _ _   3 _ _ _ _   4 _ _ _

15 (3:37) **Read aloud. Then listen and say.**

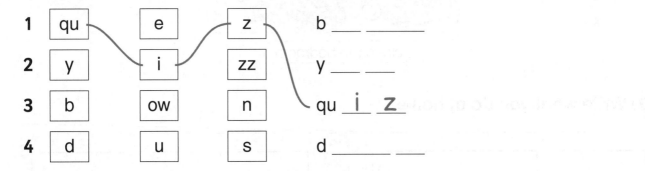

The painter is up the ladder. The pot goes down with a bump and the paint goes splat on the man. What a mess!

16 Tick (✓) the things you like to do.

1 set the table

2 wash the dishes

3 make the bed

4 wash the car

5 clean the bedroom

17 Write what you do at home.

Monday		Friday	
Tuesday		Saturday	
Wednesday		Sunday	
Thursday			

Wider World

18 **Look and write. Then draw and write about yourself.**

> do origami   play the piano   play table tennis
> do taekwondo   do ballet

1

play table tennis

2

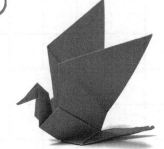

_____

3

_____

4

_____

5

_____

6

After school,

_____

19 **Ask and write.**

After-school activities

Me	Classmate 1	Classmate 2	Classmate 3

> What do you do after school?

> I play tennis.

Unit Review

20 **Look and write.**

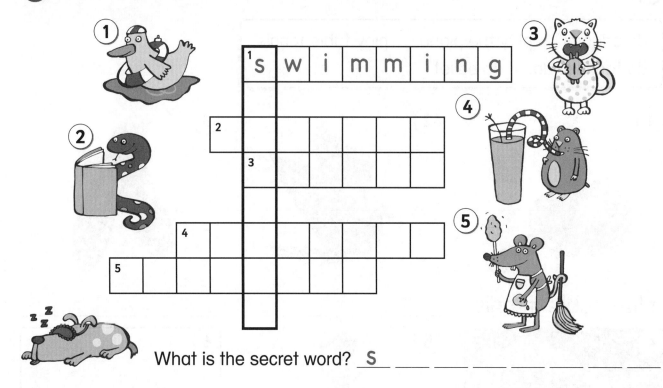

What is the secret word? _S_ ___ ___ ___ ___ ___ ___

21 **Look and write.**

What are you doing now?

1 I'm playing the piano.

2 _____

3 _____

4 _____

About Me

22 Look and write.

Talent Show

Anna

Sandy and Amy

Dan

Eddie

Mike and Fred

Gigi

1 What's Eddie doing?   He's playing the trumpet.

2 What are Sandy and Amy doing? _____

3 What's Anna doing?   _____

4 What are Mike and Fred doing? _____

5 What's Dan doing?   _____

6 What's Gigi doing?   _____

23 Draw yourself at a talent show. Describe your picture.

slowly   quickly   terribly   loudly   quietly

I'm _____ .

 I can talk about things that my friends and I are doing. ☐

I can talk about my talents. ☐

Goodbye

1 Circle the correct Quest items.

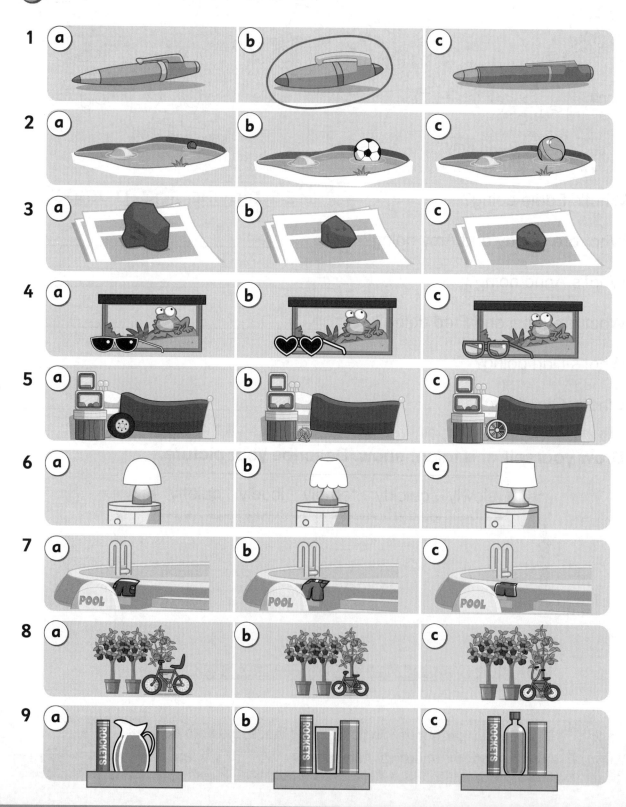

2 Write the names of the Quest items.

1 _____pen_____   2 _____   3 _____

4 _____   5 _____   6 _____

7 _____   8 _____   9 _____

3 🎧 3:44 Listen and tick (✓).

1 (a) ☐   (b) ☐   (c) ☐

2 (a) He's got big ears! ☐   (b) He's a horrible monster! ☐   (c) He's lovely! ☐

3 (a) ☐   (b) ☐   (c) ☐

4 (a) ☐   (b) ☐   (c) ☐

5 (a) ☐   (b) ☐   (c) ☐

6 (a) He can't climb! ☐   (b) He can't swim. ☐   (c) He can't dance. ☐

7 (a) green ☐   (b) red ☐   (c) yellow ☐

8 (a) ☐   (b) ☐   (c) ☐

4 **Write about the picture.**

There is a rainbow. _____

_____

_____

There are _____

_____

_____ .

5 (3:45) **Listen and tick (✓). Then write.**

☐   ☐   ☐

This is my pet _____. Its name is Pauli. It's got colourful _____

and a sharp _____ . It's got two _____ wings. It can fly

high in the _____ . It's got sharp _____ . Be careful!

6 **Write things that are in your house.**

Bedroom	Bathroom	Living room	Kitchen
bed			

7 Write about a family member or friend.

He/She can …	He/She can't …
1 _____	1 _____
2 _____	2 _____
3 _____	3 _____

8 Look and write.

__drinking__   _____   _____   _____

9 Choose and write.

I like _____

and _____ .

I don't like _____

and _____ .

My friend likes _____

and _____ .

My friend doesn't like _____

and _____ .

Halloween

1 Find, circle and write the Halloween words.

1 <u>pumpkin</u>

2 _____

3 _____

4 _____

5 _____

6 _____

7 _____

p	m	u	h	p	p	w	b	h	d	t
t	t	e	w	n	s	e	t	e	m	h
t	n	p	i	t	p	k	s	p	i	a
i	m	h	t	m	b	b	h	t	d	t
c	h	b	c	b	t	a	t	k	h	m
h	t	g	h	o	s	t	e	h	m	h
o	g	t	t	s	p	e	h	t	a	u
p	u	m	p	k	i	n	t	o	r	m
t	o	t	o	i	d	n	g	m	i	o
r	t	i	t	r	e	a	i	a	t	o
b	s	t	t	b	r	o	o	m	w	c

2 Look and write.

1 There _____is_____ _____one_____ ghost.

2 There _____ _____ witches.

3 There are _____ spiders and _____ bats.

4 There are five _____ and six _____.

Christmas Day

1 Find, circle and write the Christmas words.

1   <u>Christmas tree</u>

2   _____

3   _____

4   _____

5   _____

6   _____

7   _____

c	c	h	o	c	o	l	a	t	e	i	l	n
h	l	i	g	h	t	s	c	o	t	o	r	n
c	m	s	l	r	m	g	t	m	i	c	a	h
k	s	h	c	i	h	c	s	h	c	p	r	g
c	h	r	i	s	t	m	a	s	t	r	e	e
h	e	o	r	t	s	k	r	e	d	e	t	h
c	t	h	c	m	o	s	r	c	s	s	r	c
e	c	c	o	a	s	k	c	s	r	e	a	e
d	t	e	t	s	t	o	c	k	i	n	g	s
t	h	t	e	c	h	s	w	e	e	t	s	n
a	i	r	s	a	s	h	o	c	s	k	m	t
s	e	g	c	r	r	o	d	r	r	m	s	t
l	t	i	r	d	e	t	s	i	a	s	k	m

2 Draw a Christmas tree. Then write.

> **1** Draw the Christmas tree.   **2** Draw presents for your family.
> **3** Draw lights and sweets on your tree.   **4** Colour it.

My tree has got <u>lights</u> and _____.

There are some _____ for my family.

Easter

1 **Find and colour.**

eggs = brown   lollipops = red   baskets = yellow
bonnets = green   bunny = orange.

2 **Count and write.**

1 There are ___seven___ eggs.

2 _____ bonnets.

3 _____ lollipops.

4 _____ bunny.

3 **Make an Easter card.**

1 Decorate the egg.

2 Colour it.

3 Write Happy Easter!

April Fools' Day

1 Find, circle and write the April Fools' Day words.

1 surprise

2 _____

3 _____

4 _____

5 _____

u	s	u	r	p	r	i	s	e	i
f	k	r	j	r	f	e	n	i	s
i	r	j	a	j	o	k	e	p	r
f	f	l	t	k	o	i	l	u	k
o	a	p	r	i	l	r	n	r	e
u	s	p	i	e	n	u	i	e	r
l	o	r	b	o	i	f	r	k	i
o	s	o	k	l	s	u	r	o	r
j	k	o	a	u	p	n	j	l	o
c	c	l	o	j	k	t	o	l	o

2 Read and write.

Come to the party!

1st April

3 pm

Wear a funny hat.

Wear funny clothes.

Sam

Come _____

Tip!
Use a mirror to read this.

Review
Welcome and Unit 1

1 **Write about yourself.**

1 What's your name? _____

2 How old are you? _____

3 What's your favourite day? _____

4 When were you born? _____

2 **Write.**

1	2	3	4	5	6	7	8	9	
11	12	13	14		16		18	19	20
21	22	23	24	25		27		29	30
31		33	34	35	36	37	38		40
	42		44	45	46	47	48	49	50

3 **Write the numbers.**

1 Five plus two equals __seven__ .

2 Ten minus one equals _____.

3 Three plus twelve equals _____.

4 Eighteen minus seven equals _____.

4 **Write sentences.**

flower birds wind insects butterflies tree rainbow spiders

There's ...

1 _____ a rainbow. _____

2 _____

There are ...

1 _____

2 _____

Unit 2

1 Write the words in alphabetical order.

| eyes   moustache   hair   nose   mouth   glasses   beard   stomach   chin |

1 _____beard_____   2 _____   3 _____

4 _____   5 _____   6 _____

7 _____   8 _____   9 _____

2 Write about yourself.

| nose   hair   eyes   eyebrows   glasses   shoulders   fingernails   neck |

I've got …   I haven't got …

1 _____   1 _____

2 _____   2 _____

3 _____   3 _____

3 Write about your teacher.

1 He/She has got _____.

2 He/She hasn't got _____.

4 Ask a partner the questions. Then write the answers.

1 Have you got brown eyes?   _____

2 Have you got red hair?   _____

3 Have you got a small nose?   _____

4 Have you got thick eyebrows? _____

Unit 3

1 **Write about an animal.**

> wings   stripy   fur   soft   claws   feathers   skin
> wings   whiskers   spotty   shell   hard   sharp

It's got ...

1 _____

2 _____

3 _____

4 _____

It hasn't got ....

1 _____

2 _____

3 _____

4 _____

2 **Read and answer.**

1 Have you got a cat?   _____

2 Have you got a dog?   _____

3 Have you got a tortoise? _____

4 Have you got a bird?   _____

3 **Draw and label an animal.**

It's got _____

_____ .

It hasn't got _____

_____ .

Unit 4

1 **Write about your house.**

> there's   there isn't   there are   there aren't

1 In my bedroom _____ a wardrobe.

2 In my bathroom _____ pots.

3 In my kitchen _____ plants.

4 In my living room _____ comb.

2 **Ask your partner about their house. Write questions and answers.**

1 Is there a _____mirror_____ in your _____bathroom_____?

   _____

2 Is _____? _____

3 Are _____? _____

4 Are _____? _____

3 **Draw a room and write sentences.**

> in front of   behind   next to   above   below   opposite

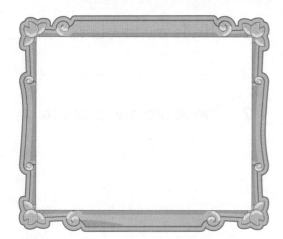

There _____.

_____

_____

_____

Unit 5

1 Write clothes words.

1 ___blouse___   2 _____   3 _____

4 _____   5 _____   6 _____

7 _____   8 _____   9 _____

2 Write about what you and your friend are wearing.

I'm wearing _____ and _____.

My friend is wearing _____ and _____.

3 Answer about yourself.

1 Are you wearing a T-shirt? _____

2 Are you wearing a belt? _____

3 Are you wearing shorts? _____

4 Are you wearing a uniform? _____

4 Draw and write about your favourite clothes.

1 This is my favourite _____

_____.

2 These are my favourite _____

_____.

Unit 6

1 **Unscramble and write.**

1 mujp __jump__   2 paly tsenni _____   3 ceabh _____

4 iudstam _____   5 myg _____   6 urn _____

7 ypal bofotall _____   8 miclb eerts   9 od adokwonet

_____   _____

2 **Write about yourself.**

I can ...   I can't ...

1 _____   1 _____

2 _____   2 _____

3 _____   3 _____

4 _____   4 _____

3 **Ask your partner about their abilities. Then write.**

He/She can ...   He/She can't ...

1 _____   1 _____

2 _____   2 _____

3 _____   3 _____

4 _____   4 _____

4 **Look and write.**

He wasn't at the _____.

He was _____

_____.

She wasn't at the _____.

She was _____

_____.

Unit 7

1 **Write the words in alphabetical order.**

> potatoes   tomatoes   carrots   cucumbers   peas   strawberries
> plums   apricots   oranges

1 ___apricots___   2 _____   3 _____

4 _____   5 _____   6 _____

7 _____   8 _____   9 _____

2 **Answer about yourself.**

1 Do you like peas?   _____

2 Do you like beans?   _____

3 Do you like tomatoes?   _____

4 Do you like oranges?   _____

3 **Write the questions.**

1 ___Do you like carrots?___? Yes, I like carrots.

2 _____? No, I don't like plums.

3 _____? No, I don't like papaya.

4 _____? Yes, I do. I love cherries.

4 **Look and answer.**

1 Is there any broccoli?   ___Yes, there is.___

2 Are there any peas?   _____

3 Is there any lettuce?   _____

4 Are there any cucumbers?   _____

Unit 8

1 **Write the questions.**

1 ___What are you doing?___ ? I'm reading.

2 _____ ? He's sleeping

3 _____ ? No, I'm not listening to music.

4 _____ ? Yes, she's reading quietly.

2 **Write the answers.**

1 Is he drinking? No, ___he isn't___ _____ .

2 Are you playing the violin? Yes, _____ .

3 Is she playing the trumpet? Yes, _____ .

4 Are you cleaning? No, _____ .

3 **Write sentences.**

doing homework   singing   playing the piano   playing the trumpet playing the flute   terribly   loudly   quickly   slowly   quietly

1 I ___`m singing loudly_____ .

2 We _____ .

3 She _____ .

4 They _____ .

5 He _____ .

4 **Match and write sentences.**

1 set   the bedroom

2 clean   the bed

3 make   the dishes

4 wash   the table

I can _____ .   I can't _____ .

Picture dictionary

Unit 1
Nature

 sun

 rock

 pond

 animal

 birds

 flowers

 insects

 mushrooms

 clouds

 trees

 ants

 worms

 spiders

 butterflies

 roses

 rainbow

 sky

wind

Places

 library

 park

 museum

 playground

Maths

 plus

 minus

 equals

Unit 2
Describing your body

small nose

black moustache

short beard

brown eyes

thick eyebrows

small glasses

red hair

grey hair

blond hair

round chin

strong chest

flat stomach

broad shoulders

strong arms

long eyelashes

long neck

short fingernails

Describing people

man

men

woman

women

people

Unit 3
Animal body parts

tail   beak   wings   feathers   claws

fins   paws   whiskers   skin   fur

Physical characteristics

spotty   stripy   soft   smooth   hard

sharp   cute   scary   fast   slow

Life cycle

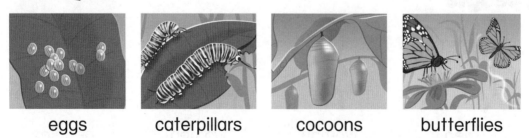

eggs   caterpillars   cocoons   butterflies

Unit 4
Furniture/Household items/Parts of the house

plant   mirror   picture   bin   wardrobe   computer

cupboard   toothbrush   toothpaste   comb   shampoo   towels

blankets   broom   plates   pots   pans   shower

garage   balcony   basement

Prepositions of place

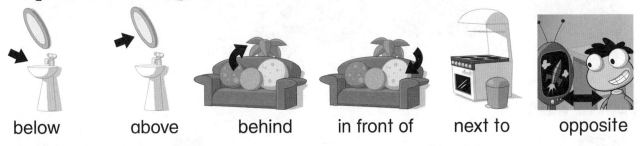

below   above   behind   in front of   next to   opposite

Materials/Shapes

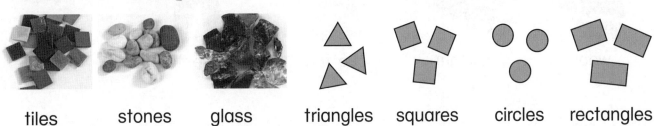

tiles   stones   glass   triangles   squares   circles   rectangles

Unit 5
Clothes

baseball hat   belt   sweatshirt   tracksuit   blouse   uniform

T-shirt   shorts   sandals   flip flops   trainers   shirt

scarf   beanie   ski jacket   woolly jumper   tights   hiking boots

Style

fancy   plain   colourful

Materials

wool   leather   cotton   polyester

Unit 6
Sports

run

ride a bike

catch a ball

play football

jump

climb trees

play tennis

play basketball

play badminton

do taekwondo

Sports/Leisure facilities

gym

basketball court

running track

stadium

skating rink

ski slope

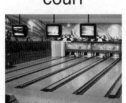
bowling alley

beach

swimming pool

football pitch

Actions

stretch your arms up

bend your knees

twist your body to the left/right

turn around

Unit 7
Food

peas

mangoes

carrots

cucumbers

plums

oranges

peaches

potatoes

tomatoes

strawberries

beans

broccoli

lettuce

spinach

cabbage

pears

apricots

avocados

cherries

watermelon

papaya

Food groups

fats and sugars

dairy

protein

cereals

fruit and vegetables

Unit 8

Actions

sleeping

reading

eating

drinking

cleaning

walking

dancing

doing homework

listening to music

making a machine

singing

playing the piano

playing the violin

playing the trumpet

playing the flute

Adverbs

quietly

loudly

quickly

slowly

terribly

Helping at home

set the table

clean the bedroom

make the bed

wash the dishes

wash the car

Pearson Education Limited
Edinburgh Gate
Harlow
Essex CM20 2JE
England
and Associated Companies throughout the world.

www.islands.pearson.com

First published 2012
Eleventh impression 2018
ISBN: 978-1-4082-9025-5

Set in Longman English 14/18
Printed in China
SWTC/11

Based on the work of Aaron Jolly and José Luis Morales

Picture Credits
The publisher would like to thank the following for their kind permission to reproduce their photographs:

(Key: b-bottom; c-centre; l-left; r-right; t-top)

15 Getty Images: Paul Mansfield Photography (1); George Doyle (2); Evan Sklar / Botanica (3). **24 Bridgeman Art Library Ltd:** Strolling along the Seashore, 1909 (oil on canvas), Sorolla y Bastida, Joaquin (1863-1923) / Museo Sorolla, Madrid, Spain / Giraudon; Self Portrait (oil on canvas), Sorolla y Bastida, Joaquin (1863-1923) / Museo Sorolla, Madrid, Spain / Index; Fritza von Riedler, 1906 (oil on canvas), Klimt, Gustav (1862-1918) / Osterreichische Galerie Belvedere, Vienna, Austria; 10 a.m., c.1938 (tempera on board), Wilson, Harry P. (fl.1938) / Laing Art Gallery, Newcastle-upon-Tyne, UK / © Tyne & Wear Archives & Museums. **35 Fotolia.com:** (b). **Shutterstock.com:** (a). **54 Fotolia.com:** (gloves, t-shirt, scarf, sandals). **Shutterstock.com:** (jumper, dress). **75 Alamy Images:** José Luis Pelaez Inc (1); dbimages (2). **iStockphoto:** (asado). **Photolibrary. com:** Imagestate (pastries). **85 Fotolia.com:** vladimir kondrachov (1); Sergey Lavrentev (4); i9370 (2); Flashon Studio (3). **Shutterstock.com:** (5). **104 Pearson Education Ltd:** Trevor Clifford (stones). **Shutterstock. com:** Voylodyon (rainbow); nikkytok (wind); Elenamiv (sky). **106 Shutterstock.com:** Viorel Sima (soft); Smit (hard); pix2go (spotty); ODM Studio (sharp); Michael Wesemann (scary); Martin Valigursky (smooth); Eric Isselée (cute, slow); David Lee (stripy); Alexandr Kolupayev (fast). **107 Alamy Images:** PhotosIndia.com LLC (toothpaste). **Fotolia.com:** Jennifer Jane (balcony); Ivonne Wierink (basement); Dmitry Naumov (shampoo); alisonhancock (garage). **Pearson Education Ltd:** Trevor Clifford (tiles, glass). **Shutterstock.com:** Tischenko Irina (broom); ruzanna (pots); Lasse Kristensen (plates); Kitch Bain (towels); Karen Miri (computer); karam Miri (blankets); Ivonne Wierink (cupboard); HD Connelly (toothbrush); Grocap (comb); Edgaras Kurauskas (pans). **108 Fotolia.com:** slyudmila (leather); matka_Wariatka (wool); Aleksandar Jocic (cotton). **Shutterstock.com:** Tatniz (plain); Margo Harrison (colourful); Lepas (scarf); Karkas (ski jacket, polyester); Iurii Konoval (beanie); igor kisselev (tights); Christophe Testi (hiking boots); Cheryl E Davis (fancy); Alexavich (woolly jumper). **109 Alamy Images:** Stadium Bank (football pitch). **Corbis:** Nik Wheeler (skating rink). **Pearson Education Ltd:** Trevor Clifford (Actions). **Shutterstock.com:** Wlg (gym); Tischenko Irina (bowling alley); Stephen Finn (stadium); J.D.S (swimming pool); goldenangel (running track); ckchiu (beach); (basketball court, ski slope). **110 Fotolia.com:** (papaya); Elena Schweitzer (watermelon). **Shutterstock.com:** Yasonya (cabbage); Valentyn Volkov (pears); Serhiy Shullye (avocados); Margrit Hirsch (lettuce); lush (apricots); Liz Van Steenburgh (brocolli); Lepas (spinach); 60126103 (cherries). **111 Corbis:** Beau Lark (wash the dishes). **Getty Images:** Jamie Grill / Iconica (clean the bedroom). **iStockphoto:** Mandygodbehear (wash the car). **Photolibrary. com:** (set the table, make the bed). Shutterstock.com: (playing the flute); MikLav (playing the piano); gemphotography (playing the trumpet); clearviewstock (singing); akva (playing the violin)

All other images © Pearson Education

Every effort has been made to trace the copyright holders and we apologise in advance for any unintentional omissions. We would be pleased to insert the appropriate acknowledgement in any subsequent edition of this publication.

Illustration Acknowledgements
Illustrated by Humberto Blanco (Sylvie Poggio Artists Agency), Anja Boretzki (Good Illustration), Chan Choi Fai, Lee Cosgrove, Leo Cultura, Marek Jagucki, Mark Ruffle (The Organisation), Yam Wai Lun, Sue King (Plum Pudding Illustration), Moreno Chiacchiera (Beehive Illustration) and HL Studios.